LETTERS OF NOTE: MUSIC

Letters of Note was born in 2009 with the launch of lettersofnote.com, a website celebrating old-fashioned correspondence that has since been visited over 100 million times. The first *Letters of Note* volume was published in October 2013, followed later that year by the first Letters Live, an event at which world-class performers delivered remarkable letters to a live audience.

Since then, these two siblings have grown side by side, with *Letters of Note* becoming an international phenomenon, and Letters Live shows being staged at iconic venues around the world, from London's Royal Albert Hall to the theatre at the Ace Hotel in Los Angeles.

You can find out more at lettersofnote.com and letterslive.com. And now you can also listen to the audio editions of the new series of *Letters of Note*, read by an extraordinary cast drawn from the wealth of talent that regularly takes part in the acclaimed Letters Live shows.

Letters of Note
Music

COMPILED BY

Shaun Usher

PENGUIN BOOKS

For Billy and Danny

PENGUIN BOOKS
An imprint of Penguin Random House LLC
penguinrandomhouse.com

First published in Great Britain by Canongate Books Ltd 2020
Published in Penguin Books 2020

Compilation and introductions copyright © 2020 by Shaun Usher
Penguin supports copyright. Copyright fuels creativity, encourages
diverse voices, promotes free speech, and creates a vibrant culture.
Thank you for buying an authorized edition of this book and for
complying with copyright laws by not reproducing, scanning,
or distributing any part of it in any form without permission.
You are supporting writers and allowing Penguin to
continue to publish books for every reader.

Pages 130–131 constitute an extension of this copyright page.

ISBN 9780143134657 (paperback)
ISBN 9780525506461 (ebook)

Printed in the United States of America
1 3 5 7 9 10 8 6 4 2

Set in Joanna MT

CONTENTS

INTRODUCTION ix

01 HE IS CALLED MICK JAGGER
Keith Richards to Aunt Patty 2

02 MY HEART ALMOST STOOD STILL
Helen Keller to the New York Symphony Orchestra 8

03 THANK YOU, AND I HOPE YOU CHOKE
Beatles fan to Nike, Inc. 12

04 I AM SO CLOSE BEHIND YOU
Leonard Cohen and Marianne Ihlen 15

05 THANK YOU
Dr Mark Taubert to David Bowie 18

06 THE GREATEST MUSICAL PLEASURE I HAVE EVER EXPERIENCED
Charles Baudelaire to Richard Wagner 26

07 I HAVE TWO HANDICAPS
Florence Price to Serge Koussevitzky 32

08 EASY, YOUNG MAN
Charles Mingus to Miles Davis 36

09 I INVENTED PUNK
Lester Bangs to *East Village Eye* magazine 42

10 COMPOSER FOR NITWTS
Erik Satie to Jean Poueigh 46

11 I HAVE LEARNT TO MASTER MYSELF
Pyotr Ilyich Tchaikovsky to Nadezhda Filaretovna von Meck 50

12 IT WASN'T A RIP OFF, IT WAS A LOVE IN
John Lennon to Craig McGregor 54

13 A GRAND SUCCESS
Lillian Nordica to her father 58

14 DO YOU STILL REMEMBER ME?
Yo-Yo Ma to Leonard Bernstein 60

15 GET AT THE VERY HEART OF IT
Ludwig van Beethoven to Emilie H. 64

16 I DON'T EVEN WRITE TO MY MOTHER
Roger Taylor to *Rolling Stone* magazine 68

17 *AIDA* WILL GATHER DUST IN THE ARCHIVES
Giuseppe Verdi, Prospero Bertani and Giulio Ricordi 70

18 PLEASE ADVISE
Teo Macero to various at Columbia Records 76

19 DON'T LET ANYONE DEFINE WHO YOU ARE
Angélique Kidjo to Girls of the World 78

20 NOT THAT ONE, DOCTOR – IT'S GOT NO RHYTHM
Richard Strauss to Hans Diestel 82

21 PICTURE THE SCENE
Rik Mayall to Bob Geldof   88

22 WHO IS KAREN CARPENTER, REALLY?
Kim Gordon to Karen Carpenter   94

23 POPPY-COCK
Harry S. Truman to Paul Hume   98

24 THE COLOR OF THE STARS, HER SKIN, HER LOVE
Jon M. Chu to Coldplay   102

25 IT'S A VIRUS
Tom Waits to *The Nation*   106

26 HERBS IS HIS MAJESTY'S
Lee 'Scratch' Perry to Tokyo's Minister of Justice   110

27 A HARMONIOUS CREATION OF ART
Adele aus der Ohe to Steinway & Sons   113

28 PLEASE CHANGE YOUR HOLD MUSIC
Dr Steven Schlozman to CVS   116

29 BLOW 'EM AWAY, KID
Nick Cave to Ptolemy   122

30 THE CREATIVE URGE
John Coltrane to Don DeMichael   125

PERMISSION CREDITS   130

ACKNOWLEDGEMENTS   132

A letter is a time bomb, a message in a bottle, a spell, a cry for help, a story, an expression of concern, a ladle of love, a way to connect through words. This simple and brilliantly democratic art form remains a potent means of communication and, regardless of whatever technological revolution we are in the middle of, the letter lives and, like literature, it always will.

INTRODUCTION

It is my great pleasure to welcome you to *Letters of Note: Music*, a journey through the letters of others. The common thread of these missives, music, is one of the few things in life to be overwhelmingly positive and profoundly enriching.

Music has the power to unite the most diverse of personalities and heal the deepest of wounds; a single note from a beloved song can transport you to a different time and lift one's mood more swiftly than the most powerful of drugs. It is no exaggeration to say that without music, were it to be outlawed today, life would have one less dimension. The only truly universal language would be lost, a means of connection would be severed, and the bonds we share would slowly weaken.

So it seems fitting to celebrate something as fundamentally important as music by way of another form of communication, the letter, the death of which, sadly, is far easier to imagine. In our ever-changing world we have surrendered to shiny new devices that promise so much, at the expense of the things that make old-fashioned correspondence so precious. The convenience of being able to tap a slab of bright glass a few times in order to send an emoji to a loved one on the other side of the world is a wonderful thing – and not one to be scoffed at – but the physical act of putting pen to paper, of carefully composing a letter, of being present and undistracted while channelling your thoughts onto the page, all for the benefit of someone else, is a powerful, satisfying, humanising act, the benefits of which are far-reaching.

It is safe to say that without music or letters, we would suffer.

So, let me be your conductor as we celebrate both forms of communication, by way of a melodic collection of letters that spans just over two centuries, beginning in 1812 and ending in 2019. Music is touched upon in letters of gratitude, anger, madness, advice, love, reassurance and joy. We shall travel to 1962, giving you a front row seat in which to enjoy the moment one of our greatest rock 'n' roll bands forged an early connection; to 1981, when one of punk's most influential critics traces the genre's birth back to unimaginable places; to 2016, to see a musical legend bid goodbye to his dear muse; to 1924, to witness the magical thank-you from a grateful deaf music fan to the orchestra she somehow 'heard'; to 1943 and the heartbreaking moment a women of colour asks a conductor to ignore both her sex and race in a bid to progress; and much more.

Whether you are a music fan or not, these letters of note will fascinate you. And should you for some unfathomable reason dislike letters, I am certain the stories and messages they contain will still enrich your life.

Switch your phones to silent, stop talking at the back, and enjoy the performance.

Shaun Usher
2020

The Letters

LETTER 01
HE IS CALLED MICK JAGGER
Keith Richards to Aunt Patty
April 1962

Since 1962 Keith Richards has been lead guitarist and songwriter in one of the most successful and influential bands of all time, a true living legend responsible for some of the most recognisable riffs in the history of rock 'n' roll. Such is the level of his fame, it is almost impossible to imagine Keith Richards prior to stardom, before he began strolling onto vast stages to thrill adoring crowds with songs that will no doubt endure for centuries to come. But thanks to a letter he once wrote to his beloved aunt, Patty, we are given such a glimpse. It was April 1962, and Keith was eighteen years old. His words brim with excitement as he describes, among other things, an encounter while awaiting the train to the London School of Economics four months earlier that would ultimately change his life. Three months after he wrote to Aunt Patty, 'The Rollin' Stones' played their first gig at the Marquee Club in London. The rest is history.

THE LETTER

> 6 Spielman Rd
> Dartford
> Kent

Dear Pat,

So sorry not to have written before (I plead insane) in bluebottle voice. Exit right amid deafening applause.

I do hope you're very well.

We have survived yet another glorious English Winter. I wonder which day Summer falls on this year?

Oh but my dear I have been soooo busy since Christmas beside working at school. You know I was keen on Chuck Berry and I thought I was the only fan for miles but one mornin' on Dartford Stn. (that's so I don't have to write a long word like station) I was holding one of Chuck's records when a guy I knew at primary school 7–11 yrs y'know came up to me. He's got every record Chuck Berry ever made and all his mates have too, they are all rhythm and blues fans, real R&B I mean (not this Dinah Shore, Brook Benton crap) Jimmy Reed, Muddy Waters, Chuck, Howlin' Wolf, John Lee Hooker all the Chicago bluesmen real lowdown stuff, marvelous. Bo Diddley he's another great.

Anyways the guy on the station, he is called Mick Jagger and all the chicks and the boys meet every Saturday morning in the 'Carousel' some juke-joint well one morning in Jan I was walking past and decided to look him up. Everybody's all over me I get invited to about 10 parties. Beside that Mick is the greatest R&B singer this side of the Atlantic and I don't mean maybe. I play guitar (electric) Chuck style we got us a bass player and drummer and rhythm-guitar and we practice 2 or 3 nights a week. SWINGIN'.

Of course they're all rolling in money and in massive detached houses, crazy, one's even got a butler. I went round there with Mick (in the car of course Mick's not mine of course) OH BOY ENGLISH IS IMPOSSIBLE.

"Can I get you anything, sir?"

"Vodka and lime, please"

"Certainly, sir"

I really felt like a lord, nearly asked for my coronet when I left.

Everything here is just fine.

I just can't lay off Chuck Berry though, I

recently got an LP of his straight from Chess Records Chicago cost me less than an English record.

Of course we've still got the old Lags here y'know Cliff Richard, Adam Faith and 2 new shockers Shane Fenton and John Leyton SUCH CRAP YOU HAVE NEVER HEARD. Except for that greaseball Sinatra ha ha ha ha ha ha ha.

Still I don't get bored anymore. This Saturday I am going to an all night party.

> "I looked at my watch
> It was four-o-five
> Man I didn't know
> If I was dead or alive"
> Quote Chuck Berry
> Reeling and a Rocking

12 galls of Beer Barrel of Cyder, 3 bottle Whiskey Wine. Her ma and pa gone away for the weekend I'll twist myself till I drop (I'm glad to say).

The Saturday after Mick and I are taking 2 girls over to our favourite Rhythm & Blues club over in Ealing, Middlesex.

They got a guy on electric harmonica Cyril

Davies fabulous always half drunk unshaven plays like a mad man, marvelous.

Well then I can't think of anything else to bore you with, so I'll sign off goodnight viewers
BIG GRIN
Luff
Keith xxxxx
Who else would write such bloody crap

'MICK IS THE GREATEST R&B SINGER THIS SIDE OF THE ATLANTIC AND I DON'T MEAN MAYBE.'
— Keith Richards

LETTER 02
MY HEART ALMOST STOOD STILL
Helen Keller to the New York Symphony Orchestra
2 February 1924

Born in Alabama in 1880, Helen Keller was yet to reach two years of age when she lost her eyesight and hearing due to an illness. Despite such a challenging start to life, she went on to do incredible things. By the age of twenty-three, having already achieved so much, her autobiography, The Story of My Life, *had been published, and over the years she travelled the world as a highly sought-after public speaker, giving eloquent lectures on all manner of topics, including her inspiring life story. As an activist, she campaigned tirelessly on behalf of the marginalised; all told, she authored a dozen books and many articles. On 2 February 1924, the morning after Beethoven's* Ninth Symphony *was performed at New York's Carnegie Hall, Keller wrote a letter of appreciation to the New York Symphony Orchestra and announced a personal breakthrough: a new-found ability to 'hear' music through touch alone, with her fingertips acting as a bridge between melodic vibrations and her mind's ear.*

THE LETTER

> 93 Seminole Avenue,
> Forest Hills, L. I.,
> February 2, 1924.

The New York Symphony Orchestra,
New York City.

Dear Friends:

I have the joy of being able to tell you that, though deaf and blind, I spent a glorious hour last night listening over the radio to Beethoven's "Ninth Symphony." I do not mean to say that I "heard" the music in the sense that other people heard it; and I do not know whether I can make you understand how it was possible for me to derive pleasure from the symphony. It was a great surprise to myself. I had been reading in my magazine for the blind of the happiness that the radio was bringing to the sightless everywhere. I was delighted to know that the blind had gained a new source of enjoyment; but I did not dream that I could have any part in their joy. Last night, when the family was listening to your wonderful rendering of the immortal symphony someone suggested that I put my hand on the receiver and see if I could get any of the vibrations. He unscrewed the cap, and I lightly touched the sensitive diaphragm. What was my amazement to discover that I could feel, not only the vibrations, but also the impassioned rhythm, the throb and the urge of the music! The intertwined and intermingling vibrations from different instruments enchanted me. I could actually distinguish the cornets, the roll of the drums, deep-toned violas and violins singing in exquisite unison. How the lovely speech of the violins flowed and plowed over the deepest tones of the other instruments! When the human voice leaped up trilling from the surge of harmony, I recognized them instantly as voices. I felt the chorus grow more exultant, more ecstatic, upcurving swift and flame-like, until my heart almost stood still. The women's voices seemed an embodiment of all the angelic voices rushing in a harmonious flood of beautiful and inspiring sound. The great chorus throbbed against my fingers with poignant pause and flow. Then all the instruments and voices together burst forth—an ocean of heavenly vibration—and died away like winds when the atom is spent, ending in a delicate shower of sweet notes.

Of course, this was not "hearing" but I do know that the tones and harmonies conveyed to me moods of great beauty and majesty. I also sensed, or thought I did, the tender sounds of nature that sing into my hand—swaying reeds and winds and the murmur of streams. I have never been so enraptured before by a multitude of tone-vibrations.

As I listened, with darkness and melody, shadow and sound filling all the room, I could not help remembering that the great composer who poured forth such a flood of sweetness into the world was deaf like myself. I marvelled at the power of his quenchless spirit by which out of his pain he wrought such joy for others—and there I sat, feeling with my hand the magnificent symphony which broke like a sea upon the silent shores of his soul and mine.

Let me thank you warmly for all the delight which your beautiful music has brought to my household and to me. I want also to thank Station WEAF for the joy they are broadcasting in the world.

With kindest regards and best wishes, I am,
Sincerely yours,
[Signed]
HELEN KELLER

LETTER 03
THANK YOU, AND I HOPE YOU CHOKE
Beatles fan to Nike, Inc.
30 March 1987

In March 1987, a black-and-white Nike Air advert appeared on television that was unremarkable but for one detail: its soundtrack had been plucked from the sacred back catalogue of one of history's most recognisable bands, The Beatles. It was the first time that one of the Fab Four's songs had been used for such a purpose. To complicate matters, the surviving Beatles were unaware: its usage had been cleared, in part, by John Lennon's widow, Yoko Ono, seemingly without consultation. Unsurprisingly, a messy lawsuit soon reared its head, a many-limbed beast that persisted for two long years before finally being put to rest in 1989, out of court. The advert was banished for ever. Much swifter, however, was the retribution served by a furious Beatles fan by way of this letter, sent to Nike's advertising department shortly after the advert first aired. The letter, I am told, now hangs at the company's head office.

THE LETTER

March 30, 1987

Nike, Inc.
Advertising/Marketing Dept.
3900 SW Murray
Beverton, OR 97005

Dear Sir or Madam:

This letter of complaint is in response to a very nauseating advertisement of yours which I saw on television yesterday. From your complete lack of taste you have created a commercial for your "Michael Jordan" shoes which exploits, defiles and utterly insults Beatles' fans, and all others of musical distinction. Your debasement of the Beatles' song, "Revolution", in the commercial ad is apparently indicative of your lack of integrity as a business. Your tactic, obviously, is to use the Beatles' universal popularity to sell your product. Have you sunk that low? "Is nothing sacred anymore?", as the cliché goes? Your only motive is to make more money for your greedy selves, and in the process you seemingly could not care less that you have trampled and befouled the precious memories of millions and millions of people throughout the entire world. Your kind makes me puke; you low, vacuous, malodorous perverts. Your dearth of sensitivity is equaled only by your plethora of obnoxiousness. To your credit, you have waited nearly seven years since the death of John Ono Lennon; but it was obviously not done out of respect (Huh? What's that?) for the deceased.

Throughout my high school years as a basketball player, on to my college years, and up to the present day, I have bought your athletic shoes. However, as of this very day, I can assure you that I, and many of my friends, will never, EVER, contribute in any way whatsoever to your sickeningly corporate-selling tactics. You know, with people like you in the world, euthanasia has untapped possibilities.

Thank you, and I hope you choke.

Very untruly yours.

LETTER 04
I AM SO CLOSE BEHIND YOU
Leonard Cohen and Marianne Ihlen
2016

In 1960 Leonard Cohen moved from Montreal to Hydra, a peaceful Greek island on which he would live intermittently for the next seven years and write a collection of poetry and two novels. Soon after arriving, he met and fell for Marianne Ihlen, a twenty-three-year-old Norwegian woman who had been on the island since arriving in 1958 with her husband, who had since abandoned her and their young son. The relationship blossomed. Ihlen became Cohen's muse and she inspired, among other songs, 1967's 'So Long, Marianne'. But they eventually grew apart, and by the 1970s they had moved on. Decades later, in 2016, upon hearing that Ihlen's health was failing and she had very little time left, Cohen wrote her a farewell letter. A reply soon arrived. Just a few months after her death, Cohen also passed away.

THE LETTERS

Well Marianne, it's come to this time when we are really so old and our bodies are falling apart and I think I will follow you very soon. Know that I am so close behind you that if you stretch out your hand, I think you can reach mine.

And you know that I've always loved you for your beauty and your wisdom, but I don't need to say anything more about that because you know all about that. But now, I just want to wish you a very good journey.

Goodbye old friend. Endless love, see you down the road.

* * *

Dear Leonard,
Marianne slept slowly out of this life yesterday evening. Totally at ease, surrounded by close friends.

Your letter came when she still could talk and laugh in full consciousness. When we read it aloud, she smiled as only Marianne can. She lifted her hand, when you said you were right behind, close enough to reach her.

It gave her deep peace of mind that you knew her condition. And your blessing for the journey gave her extra strength. Jan and her friends who saw what this message meant for her, will all thank you in deep gratitude for replying so fast and with such love and compassion.

In her last hour I held her hand and hummed Bird on a Wire, while she was breathing so lightly. And when we left the room, after her soul had flown out of the window for new adventures, we kissed her head and whispered your everlasting words

So long, Marianne

LETTER 05
THANK YOU
Dr Mark Taubert to David Bowie
January 2016

On 10 January 2016, two days after the release of David Bowie's latest album, Blackstar, millions of hearts around the world broke with the news of Bowie's death following an eighteen-month battle with cancer. Bowie was a true visionary, the like of whom appears once in a generation at most, and his impact on the world of music was, and remains, immense. That he planned for his final album to be released so close to his last breath makes perfect sense. For this was his goodbye. Five days later, Bowie's son shared a letter of thanks that had been written to David Bowie by Dr Mark Taubert, a palliative care consultant working for the Velindre University NHS Trust in Cardiff.

THE LETTER

Dear David,

Oh no, don't say it's true – whilst realization of your death was sinking in during those grey, cold January days of 2016, many of us went on with our day jobs. At the beginning of that week I had a discussion with a hospital patient, facing the end of her life. We discussed your death and your music, and it got us talking about numerous weighty subjects, that are not always straightforward to discuss with someone facing their own demise. In fact, your story became a way for us to communicate very openly about death, something many doctors and nurses struggle to introduce as a topic of conversation. But before I delve further into the aforementioned exchange, I'd like to get a few other things off my chest, and I hope you don't find them a saddening bore.

Thank you for the Eighties when your *ChangesOneBowie* album provided us with hours of joyful listening, in particular on a trip from Darmstadt to Cologne and back. My friends and I will probably always associate Diamond Dogs, Rebel Rebel, China Girl and Golden Years with that particular time in our lives. Needless to say, we had a great time in Köln.

Thank you for Berlin, especially early on, when your songs provided some of the musical backdrop to what was happening in East and West Germany. I still have *Helden* on vinyl and played it again when I heard you had died (you'll be pleased to hear that Helden will also feature in our next Analogue Music Club in the Pilot pub in Penarth later this month). Some may associate David Hasselhoff with the fall of the wall and reunification; but many Germans probably wish that time had taken a cigarette and put it in Mr Hasselhoff's mouth around that time, rather than hear *I've been looking for freedom* endlessly on the radio. For me that time in our history is sound tracked by 'Heroes'.

Thanks also on behalf of my friend Ifan, who went to one of your gigs in Cardiff. His sister Haf was on the doors that night and I heard a rumour that Ifan managed to sneak in for free (he says sorry!). You gave him and his mate a wave from the stage which will remain in his memory forever.

Thank you for Lazarus and Blackstar. I am a palliative care doctor, and what you have done in the time surrounding your death has had a profound effect on me and many people I work with. Your album is strewn with references, hints and allusions. As always, you don't make interpretation all that easy, but perhaps that isn't the point. I have often heard how meticulous you were in your life. For me, the fact that your gentle death at home coincided so closely with the release of your album, with its good-bye message, in my mind is unlikely to be coincidence. All of this was carefully planned, to become a work of death art. The video of Lazarus is very deep and many of the scenes will mean different things to us all; for me it is about dealing with the past when you are faced with inevitable death.

Your death at home. Many people I talk to as part of my job think that death predominantly happens in hospitals, in very clinical settings, but I presume you chose home and planned this in some detail. This is one of our aims in palliative care, and your ability to achieve this may mean that others will see it as an option they would like fulfilled. The photos that emerged of you some days after your death, were said to be from the last weeks of your life. I do not know whether this is correct, but I am certain that many of us would like to carry off a sharp suit in the same way that you did in those photos. You looked great, as always, and it seemed in direct defiance of all the scary monsters that the last weeks of life can be associated with.

For your symptom control needs, you will presumably have had palliative care professionals advise on pain, nausea, vomiting, breathlessness, and I can imagine they did this well. I envisage that they also discussed any emotional anguish you may have had.

For your advance care planning (i.e. planning health and care decisions ahead of things getting worse and before becoming unable to express them), I am certain you will have had a lot of ideas, expectations, prior decisions and stipulations. These may have been set out clearly in writing, near your bed at home, so that everyone who met you was clear on what you wanted, regardless of your ability to communicate. It is an area not just palliative care professionals, but in fact all healthcare workers want to provide and improve, so that it is less likely that any sudden health incidents will automatically result in a blue-light ambulance emergency room admission. Especially when people become unable to speak for themselves.

And I doubt that anyone will have given you Cardiopulmonary Resuscitation (CPR) in the last hours/days of your life, or even considered it. Regrettably, some patients who have not actively opted out of this treatment still receive it, by default. It involves physical, sometimes bone-breaking chest compressions, electric shocks, injections and insertion of airways and is only successful in 1–2% of patients whose cancer has spread to other organs in their body. It is very likely that you asked your medical team to issue you with a Do Not Attempt Cardiopulmonary Resuscitation order. This is something we try to offer here in Wales, as part of the Talk CPR campaign for people with palliative illness. I can only imagine what it must have been like to discuss this, but you were once again a hero, or a 'Held', even at this most challenging time of your life.

And the professionals who saw you will have had good knowledge and skill in the provision of palliative and end-of-life care. Sadly, this essential part of training is not always available for junior healthcare professionals, including doctors and nurses, and is sometimes overlooked or under-prioritized by those who plan their education. I think if you were ever to return (as Lazarus did), you would be a firm advocate for good palliative care training being available everywhere.

So back to the conversation I had with the lady who had recently received the news that she had advanced cancer that had spread, and that she would probably not live much longer than a year or so. She talked about you and loved your music, but for some reason was not impressed by your Ziggy Stardust outfit (she was not sure whether you were a boy or a girl). She too, had memories of places and events for which you provided an idiosyncratic soundtrack. And then we talked about a good death, the dying moments and what these typically look like. And we talked about palliative care and how it can help. She told me about her mother's and her father's death, and that she wanted to be at home when things progressed, not in a hospital or emergency room, but that she'd happily transfer to the local hospice should her symptoms be too challenging to treat at home.

We both wondered who may have been around you when you took your last breath and whether anyone was holding your hand. I believe this was an aspect of the vision she had of her own dying moments that was of utmost importance to her, and you gave her a way of expressing this most personal longing to me, a relative stranger.

Thank you.

'THANK YOU FOR LAZARUS AND BLACKSTAR. I AM A PALLIATIVE CARE DOCTOR, AND WHAT YOU HAVE DONE IN THE TIME SURROUNDING YOUR DEATH HAS HAD A PROFOUND EFFECT ON ME AND MANY PEOPLE I WORK WITH.'

— Dr Mark Taubert

LETTER 06
THE GREATEST MUSICAL PLEASURE I HAVE EVER EXPERIENCED
Charles Baudelaire to Richard Wagner
17 February 1860

In 1849, as a result of his political activism, German composer Richard Wagner was forced to flee his country of birth and live in Switzerland, Venice and then France. In total, he remained in exile for thirteen years. It was during this period of uncertainty, shortly before he returned to Germany, that Wagner conducted a number of concerts at a Parisian theatre known as the Salle Ventadour. One member of the audience who was particularly taken with the shows, despite having been previously unfamiliar with Wagner's work, was noted French poet Charles Baudelaire. In fact, he was so impressed by what he deemed 'the greatest musical pleasure [he had] ever experienced' that a few days after the last performance he wrote Wagner a letter.

THE LETTER

Dear Sir:

I have always imagined that however used to fame a great artist may be, he cannot be insensible to a sincere compliment, especially when that compliment is like a cry of gratitude; and finally that this cry could acquire a singular kind of value when it came from a Frenchman, which is to say from a man little disposed to be enthusiastic, and born, moreover, in a country where people hardly understand painting and poetry any better than they do music. First of all, I want to tell you that I owe you the greatest musical pleasure I have ever experienced. I have reached an age when one no longer makes it a pastime to write letters to celebrities, and I should have hesitated a long time before writing to express my admiration for you, if I did not daily come across shameless and ridiculous articles in which every effort is made to libel your genius. You are not the first man, sir, about whom I have suffered and blushed for my country. At length indignation impelled me to give you an earnest of my gratitude; I said to myself, "I want to stand out from all those imbeciles."

The first time I went to the Italian Theatre in order to hear your works, I was rather unfavorably disposed and indeed, I must admit, full of nasty prejudices, but I have an excuse: I have been so often duped; I have heard so much music by pretentious charlatans. But you conquered me at once. What I felt is beyond description, and if you will be kind enough not to laugh, I shall try to interpret it for you. At the outset it seemed to me that I knew this new music, and later, on thinking it over, I understood whence came this mirage; it seemed to me that this music was mine, and I recognized it in the way that any man recognizes the things he is destined to love. To anybody but an intelligent man, this statement would be immensely ridiculous, especially when it comes from one who, like me, does not know music, and whose whole education consists in having heard (most pleasurably, to be sure) some few fine pieces by Weber and Beethoven.

Next, the thing that struck me the most was the character of grandeur. It depicts what is grand and incites to grandeur. Throughout your works I found again the solemnity of the grand sounds of Nature in her grandest aspects, as well as the solemnity of the grand passions of man. One feels immediately carried away and dominated. One of the strangest pieces, which indeed gave me a new musical sensation, is the one intended to depict a religious ecstasy. The effect produced by the *Entrance of the Guests* and the *Wedding Fête* is tremendous. I felt in it all the majesty of a larger life than ours. Another thing: quite often I experienced a sensation of a rather bizarre nature, which was the pride and the joy of understanding, of letting myself be penetrated and invaded — a really sensual delight that resembles that of rising in the air or tossing upon the sea. And the music at the same time would now and then resound with the pride of life. Generally these profound harmonies seemed to me like those stimulants that quicken the pulse of the imagination. Finally, and I entreat you not to laugh, I also felt sensations which probably derive from my own turn of mind and my most frequent concerns. There is everywhere something rapt and enthralling, something aspiring to mount higher, something excessive and superlative. For example, if I may make analogies with painting, let me suppose I have before me a vast expanse of dark red. If this red stands for passion, I see it gradually passing through all the transitions of red and pink to the incandescent glow of a furnace. It would seem difficult, impossible even, to reach anything more glowing; and yet a last fuse comes and traces a whiter streak on the white of the background. This will signify, if you will, the supreme utterance of a soul at its highest paroxysm.

I had begun to write a few meditations on the pieces from *Tannhäuser* and *Lohengrin* that we listened to; but soon saw the impossibility of saying everything. Similarly, this letter could go on interminably. If you have been able to read it through, I thank you. It only remains for me to add a few words. From the day when I heard your music, I have said to myself endlessly, and especially at bad times, "If I only could hear a little Wagner tonight!" There are doubtless other men constituted like myself. After all, you must have been pleased with the public, whose instinct proved far superior to the false science of the journalists. Why not give us a few more concerts, adding some new pieces? You have given us a foretaste of new delights – have you the right to withhold the rest? Once again, sir, I thank you; you brought me back to myself and to what is great, in some unhappy moments.

Ch. Baudelaire

I do not set down my address because you might think I wanted something from you.

'I HAVE HEARD SO
MUCH MUSIC BY
PRETENTIOUS
CHARLATANS. BUT
YOU CONQUERED
ME AT ONCE.'
— Charles Baudelaire

LETTER 07
I HAVE TWO HANDICAPS
Florence Price to Serge Koussevitzky
5 July 1943

Florence Price was born in 1887 in Little Rock, and by the tender age of four, guided by her mother, who was a music teacher, she had played her first piano recital. Her love of all things musical only intensified with time, and by adulthood she was immersed in the overwhelmingly white and male world of classical music. In 1933, despite her race and gender, Price made history when her piece, Symphony in E Minor, *became the first composition written by an African-American woman to be played not only by the Chicago Symphony Orchestra, but any major orchestra. Frustratingly, this was not the norm, and Price spent much of her career proactively searching for a route through to audiences. In 1943 she wrote to Serge Koussevitzky, the revered conductor who led the Boston Symphony Orchestra for twenty-five years, and asked him to consider using one of her scores. In this instance, as with many, her plea fell on deaf ears.*

THE LETTER

My dear Dr. Koussevitzky,

To begin with I have two handicaps—those of sex and race. I am a woman; and I have some Negro blood in my veins.

Knowing the worst, then, would you be good enough to hold in check the possible inclination to regard a woman's composition as long on emotionalism but short on virility and thought content;—until you shall have examined some of my work?

As to the handicap of race, may I relieve you by saying that I neither expect nor ask any concession on that score. I should like to be judged on merit alone—the great trouble having been to get conductors, who know nothing of my work (I am practically unknown in the East, except perhaps as the composer of two songs, one or the other of which Marian Anderson includes on most of her programs) to even consent to examine a score.

I confess that I am woefully lacking in the hardihood of aggression; that writing this letter to you is the result of having successfully done battle with a hounding timidity.

Having been born in the South and having spent most of my childhood there I believe I can truthfully say that I understand the real Negro music. In some of my work I make use of the idiom undiluted. Again, at other times it merely flavors my themes. And at still other times thoughts come in the garb of the other side of my mixed racial background. I have tried for practical purposes to cultivate and preserve a facility of expression in both idioms, altho I have an unwavering and compelling faith that a national music very beautiful and very American can come from the melting pot just as the nation itself has done.

Will you examine one of my scores?
Yours very sincerely,
[Signed Florence B. Price]

'I HAVE AN UNWAVERING AND COMPELLING FAITH THAT A NATIONAL MUSIC VERY BEAUTIFUL AND VERY AMERICAN CAN COME FROM THE MELTING POT JUST AS THE NATION ITSELF HAS DONE.'

— Florence B. Price

**LETTER 08
EASY, YOUNG MAN**
Charles Mingus to Miles Davis
30 November 1955

*In early November 1955, American jazz magazine
DownBeat published 'Miles: A Trumpeter in the Midst of
a Big Comeback Makes a Very Frank Appraisal of
Today's Jazz Scene', a remarkably candid interview with
esteemed jazz trumpeter and composer Miles Davis in
which he took aim at numerous fellow musicians,
including renowned double bassist and composer
Charles Mingus, another giant in the world of jazz
who had just recently played on – and published on his
own label – Davis's album,* Blue Moods. *Rather than
ignore Davis's charge that his arrangements were
'depressing' and 'tired modern paintings', Mingus chose
to respond with a letter that was soon reprinted in
DownBeat.*

THE LETTER

Four editions of Down Beat come to my mind's eye—Bird's "Blindfold Test," mine, Miles', and Miles' recent "comeback story"—as I sit down and attempt to honestly write my thoughts in an open letter to Miles Davis. (I discarded numerous "mental" letters before this writing, but one final letter formed last night as I looked through some pictures of Bird that Bob Parent had taken at a Village session.) If a picture needs to go with this story, it should be this picture of Bird, standing and looking down at Monk with more love than I think we'll ever find in this jazz business! . . .

Bird's love, so warmly obvious in this picture, was again demonstrated in his "Blindfold Test." But dig Miles' "Test"! As a matter of fact, dig my own "Blindfold Test"! See what I mean? And more recently, dig Miles' comeback story. How is Miles going to act when he gets back and gets going again? Will it be like a gig in Brooklyn not too long ago with Max, Monk, and me when he kept telling Monk to "lay out" because his chords were all wrong? Or even at a more recent record date when he cursed, laid out, argued, and threatened Monk and asked Bob Weinstock why he hired such a nonmusician and would Monk lay out on his trumpet solos? What's happening to us disciples of Bird? Or would Miles think I'm presuming too much to include myself as one?

It seems so hard for some of us to grow up mentally just enough to realize there are other persons of flesh and bone, just like us, on this great, big earth. And if they don't ever stand still, move, or "swing," they are as right as we are, even if they are as wrong as hell by our standards. Yes, Miles, I am apologizing for my stupid "Blindfold Test." I can do it gladly because I'm learning a little something. No matter how much they try to say that Brubeck doesn't swing—or whatever else they're stewing or whoever else they're brewing—it's factually unimportant.

Not because Dave made Time magazine—and a dollar—but mainly because Dave honestly thinks he's swinging. He feels a certain pulse and plays a certain pulse which gives him pleasure and a sense of exaltation because he's sincerely doing something the way he, Dave Brubeck, feels like doing it. And as you said in your story, Miles, "if a guy makes you pat your foot, and if you feel it down your back, etc.," then Dave is the swingingest by your definition, Miles, because at Newport and elsewhere Dave had the whole house patting its feet and even clapping its hands . . .

Miles, don't you remember that "Mingus Fingers" was written in 1945 when I was a youngster, 22 years of age, who was studying and doing his damnedest to write in the Ellington tradition? Miles, that was 10 years ago when I weighed 185. Those clothes are worn and don't fit me anymore. I'm a man; I weigh 215; I think my own way. I don't think like you and my music isn't meant just for the patting of feet and going down backs. When and if I feel gay and carefree, I write or play that way—or when I'm happy, or depressed, even.

Just because I'm playing jazz I don't forget about me. I play or write me the way I feel through jazz, or whatever. Music is, or was, a language of the emotions. If someone has been escaping reality, I don't expect him to dig my music, and I would begin to worry about my writing if such a person began to really like it. My music is alive and it's about the living and the dead, about good and evil. It's angry yet it's real because it knows it's angry.

I know you're making a comeback, Miles, and I'm with you more than you know. You're playing the greatest Miles I've ever heard, and I'm sure you already know that you're one of America's truly great jazz stylists. You're often fresh in a creative sense and, if anything, you underevaluate yourself—on the outside—and so with other associates in the art. Truly, Miles, I love you and want you to know you're needed here, but you're too important a person in jazz to be less than extra careful about what you say about other musicians who are also trying to create . . .

Remember me, Miles? I'm Charles. Yeah, Mingus! You read third trumpet on my California record dates 11 years ago on the recommendation of Lucky Thompson. So easy, young man. Easy on those stepping stones . . .

If you should get around to answering this open letter, Miles, there is one thing I would like to know concerning what you said to Nat Hentoff about all the tunes you've recorded in the last two years. Why did you continue to record, session after session, when you now say you didn't like them except for two LPs? I wonder if you forgot the names of those tunes; also, how a true artist can allow all this music, which even he himself doesn't like, to be sold to the jazz public. Or even accept payment for a job which you yourself say wasn't well done.

Good luck on your comeback, Miles.

'MY MUSIC IS ALIVE AND IT'S ABOUT THE LIVING AND THE DEAD, ABOUT GOOD AND EVIL. IT'S ANGRY YET IT'S REAL BECAUSE IT KNOWS IT'S ANGRY.'

– Charles Mingus

LETTER 09
I INVENTED PUNK
Lester Bangs to *East Village Eye* magazine
1981

Nearly forty years since his untimely death in 1982 at the age of thirty-three, Lester Bangs retains the reputtion he earned during his brief but impactful life – as one of popular music's most eloquent and outspoken critics. A native of Southern California, Bangs began his professional career writing reviews for Rolling Stone, *but soon moved to Detroit to work full-time for* Creem *magazine, where his distinctive style came to define that publication's irreverent attitude and tone. An early champion of the 1970s punk movement, Bangs oversaw its evolution during the latter part of the decade after moving to New York City, where he continued to chronicle rock's fables and foibles until his sudden passing from an unintended drug overdose. In 1981, tiring of the seemingly endless debates over its origins, he wrote this letter to the* East Village Eye *wherein, with his characteristic blend of passion and cynicism, Bangs put to rest a question on the lips of many: Who invented punk?*

THE LETTER

Dear East Village Eye:
So far in your pages I have at different times learned that both Richard Hell and John Holmstrom invented punk, presumably also at different times. So I figured I might as well put my two cents' worth in. I invented punk. Everybody knows that. But I stole it from Greg Shaw, who also invented power pop. And he stole it from Dave Marsh, who actually saw Question Mark and the Mysterians live once. But he stole it from John Sinclair. Who stole it from Rob Tyner. Who stole it from Iggy. Who stole it from Lou Reed. Who stole it from Gene Vincent. Who stole it from James Dean. Who stole it from Marlon Brando. Who stole it from Robert Mitchum. The look on his face in the photo when he got busted for grass. And he stole it from Humphrey Bogart. Who stole it from James Cagney. Who stole it from Pretty Boy Floyd. Who stole it from Harry Crosby. Who stole it from Teddy Roosevelt. Who stole it from Billy the Kid. Who stole it from Mike Fink. Who stole it from Stonewall Jackson. Who stole it from Napoleon. Who stole it from Voltaire. Who stole it from an anonymous wino whose pocket he once picked while the man was lying comatose in a Paris gutter,

you writers know how it gets when you're waiting on those royalty checks. The wino stole it from his mother, a toothless hag who once turned tricks till she got too old and ugly whereupon she became a seamstress except she wasn't very good, her palsied hands shook so bad all her seams were loosely threaded and dresses would fall off elegant Parisian women right in the middle of the street. Which is how Lady Godiva happened. Lady Godiva was a punk too, she stole it from the hag to get revenge. And Godiva's horse stole it from her. Soon thereafter said horse was ridden off to battle where it died, but not before the Major astride the horse stole punk from it. The Major was a serious alcoholic given to extensive periods of blackout running into weeks and even months, so he forgot he stole it. He forgot he ever had it. Forgot what it ever was or meant. Just like all of us. But one night in a drunken stupor he burbled out the age-old and Grail-priceless Secret of Punk to another alkie with a better memory. When the Major sobered up, the other alkie, a pickpocket and generalized petty thief, lied and told the Major that he, the pickpocket, had originally owned punk but that one night when he, the pickpocket, was in his cups the Major stole punk from him. The Major believed this. But later he got drunk and forgot all about punk again. So it might have been lost in one of the crevasses of history and John Holmstrom would be an aluminum-siding salesman door-to-door and Richard Hell would be pitching hay down from the loft of some midwestern farm where he was hired hand RIGHT AT THIS VERY MOMENT in which also I, creator of punk as I really shouldn't have to remind you, would not be a rock critic and sometime musician to the irritation of many and pleasure of some enlightened folk but rather a senior poobah in the headquarters of Jehovah's Witnesses over in Brooklyn. Instead of reviewing Devo from the Voice I would be the author of the article "Springs—the Wonder Metal," published in *Awake!* magazine sometime in 1978. And that too would be something to be proud of.

Lester Bangs

LETTER 10
COMPOSER FOR NITWITS
Erik Satie to Jean Poueigh
1917

Eccentric. Weird. Unusual. All words regularly used to describe both the character and work of Erik Satie, a celebrated French pianist of limited technical expertise whose compositions attracted attention far and wide thanks to their offbeat angular jaunty nature and their overriding brilliance. When it came to accepting criticism, however, Satie was less successful. On 18 May 1917 a ballet named Parade premiered at the Théâtre du Châtelet in Paris, with music by Satie, writing by Jean Cocteau and set design courtesy of Pablo Picasso. Much to Satie's annoyance, this impressive roster of talent somehow failed to rescue the show from a savaging by Jean Poueigh, a music critic with whom Satie had shaken hands after the event. Having read the review, and feeling particularly betrayed after their fleeting contact, Satie wrote him a note. And then he sent another. And then another. Sensibly, Poueigh remained silent, instead choosing to sue Satie for slander. The composer was sentenced to eight days in jail for his troubles, and Cocteau was arrested for screaming obscenities in the courtroom.

THE LETTERS

> 30 May 1917
> To Jean Poueigh

Sir and dear friend,
What I know is that you are an ass-hole, and, if I dare say so, an unmusical ass-hole. Above all, never again offer me your dirty hand.
 Erik Satie

* * *

> 3 June 1917

To Monsieur Jean Poueigh, Head Flop, Chief Gourds and Turkey
You are not as dumb as I thought. Despite your bonehead air and your short-sightedness, you see things at a great distance.
 Erik Satie

* * *

5 June 1917

To Monsieur Fuckface Poueigh, Famous Pumpkin
and Composer for Nitwits
Lousy ass-hole, this is from where I shit on you
with all my force.
   Erik Satie

'WHAT I KNOW IS THAT YOU ARE AN ASS-HOLE, AND, IF I DARE SAY SO, AN UNMUSICAL ASS-HOLE.'

— Erik Satie

LETTER 11
I HAVE LEARNT TO MASTER MYSELF
Pyotr Ilyich Tchaikovsky to Nadezhda Filaretovna von Meck
5 March 1878

For thirteen years, Pyotr Ilyich Tchaikovsky was able to commit himself fully to composing the operas, ballets, concertos and symphonies for which he is now rightly celebrated, thanks in no small part to the generosity of one person: Nadezhda Filaretovna von Meck. Von Meck was a music-loving Russian businesswoman turned patron of the arts whose vast fortune allowed her to support Tchaikovsky financially from 1877, thus freeing him from the stresses of everyday life. Remarkably, the two never met in person; however, they corresponded frequently and became close friends through the page, their letters offering Tchaikovsky a sorely needed opportunity to ruminate freely and passionately about his music and his life. This was just one of those times.

THE LETTER

Clarens, March 5th, 1878.

It is delightful to talk to you about my own methods of composition. So far I have never had any opportunity of confiding to anyone these hidden utterances of my inner life; partly because very few would be interested, and partly because, of these few, scarcely one would know how to respond to me properly. To you, and you alone, I gladly describe all the details of the creative process, because in you I have found one who has a fine feeling and can understand my music.

Do not believe those who try to persuade you that composition is only a cold exercise of the intellect. The only music capable of moving and touching us is that which flows from the depths of a composer's soul when he is stirred by inspiration. There is no doubt that even the greatest musical geniuses have sometimes worked without inspiration. This guest does not always respond to the first invitation. We must *always* work, and a self-respecting artist must not fold his hands on the pretext that he is not in the mood. If we wait for the mood, without endeavouring to meet it halfway, we easily become indolent and apathetic.

We must be patient, and believe that inspiration will come to those who can master their *disinclination*. A few days ago I told you I was working every day without any real inspiration. Had I given way to my disinclination, undoubtedly I should have drifted into a long period of idleness. But my patience and faith did not fail me, and to-day I felt that inexplicable glow of inspiration of which I told you; thanks to which I know beforehand that whatever I write to-day will have power to make an impression, and to touch the hearts of those who hear it. I hope you will not think I am indulging in self-laudation, if I tell you that I very seldom suffer from this disinclination to work. I believe the reason for this is that I am naturally patient. I have learnt to master myself, and I am glad I have not followed in the steps of some of my Russian colleagues, who have no self-confidence and are so impatient that at the least difficulty they are ready to throw up the sponge. This is why, in spite of great gifts, they accomplish so little, and that in an amateur way.

You ask me how I manage my instrumentation. I never compose in the *abstract*; that is to say, the musical thought never appears otherwise than in a suitable external form. In this way I invent the musical idea and the instrumentation simultaneously.

Thus I thought out the scherzo of our symphony—at the moment of its composition—exactly as you heard it. It is inconceivable except as *pizzicato*. Were it played with the bow, it would lose all its charm and be a mere body without a soul.

As regards the Russian element in my works, I may tell you that not infrequently I begin a composition with the intention of introducing some folk-melody into it. Sometimes it comes of its own accord, unintentionally (as in the finale of our symphony). As to this national element in my work, its affinity with the folksongs in some of my melodies and harmonies proceeds from my having spent my childhood in the country, and having, from my earliest years, been impregnated with the characteristic beauty of our Russian folk-music. I am passionately fond of the national element in all its varied expressions. In a word, I am Russian in the fullest sense of the word.

LETTER 12
IT WASN'T A RIP OFF, IT WAS A LOVE IN
John Lennon to Craig McGregor
14 September 1971

On 14 June 1970, shortly after the break-up of The Beatles, an article by journalist Craig McGregor appeared on page thirteen of the New York Times *titled 'So in the End, the Beatles Have Proved False Prophets', in which the band were labelled as 'white imitators of black music' who 'exploited the black man's music and finally betrayed it' by churning out increasingly conventional, safe and 'counter-revolutionary' songs. Perhaps it took fifteen months for a copy of the piece to reach him, or maybe digesting such a charge was simply a slow process, but it took until September of the next year, at which point he was aboard an American Airlines aircraft, for John Lennon to respond by letter to McGregor, handwritten on a couple of sheets of in-flight stationery.*

THE LETTER

American Airlines

In Flight . . . yes
Altitude . . . puzzled.
Location . . . yes.

14th Sep. 71.

Dear Craig McGregor
'Money', 'Twist 'n' Shout', 'You really got a hold on me' etc, were all numbers we (the Beatles) used to sing in the dancehalls around Britain, mainly Liverpool. It was only natural that we tried to do it <u>as near to</u> the record as we could — i always wished we could have done them even closer to the original. We didn't sing our own songs in the early days — really weren't good enough — the one thing we <u>always did</u> was to <u>make it known</u> that there were <u>black originals</u>, we <u>loved</u> the music and wanted to spread it in <u>any way we could</u>. In the '50s there were few people listening to blues — R & B — rock and roll, in America as well as Britain. People like — Eric Burdon's Animals — Mick's Stones — and us drank ate and slept the music, and also <u>recorded it</u>, many kids were turned on to black music by us.

It wasnt a rip off
it was a love in

John + Yennon

P.S. what about the 'B' side of 'Money'?
P.P.S. even the black kids didn't dig blues etc, it wasn't 'sharp' or something.

'WE <u>LOVED</u> THE MUSIC AND WANTED TO SPREAD IT IN <u>ANY WAY WE COULD</u>.'

– John Lennon

LETTER 13
A GRAND SUCCESS
Lillian Nordica to her father
13 May 1879

In April 1879, at the Teatro Guillaume in Brescia, Italy, American soprano Lillian Nordica made her operatic debut in Giuseppe Verdi's La traviata, *in the lead role of Violetta. The next month, buoyed enormously by the rave reviews that had met her first foray into the world of opera, Nordica proudly wrote home to her father.*

THE LETTER

May 3, 1879

Dear Father:

Mother has written, I suppose at some length, on my great success in opera. Well, she cannot say too much. I have had a grand success and no mistake. Such yelling and shouting you never heard. The theatre is packed. I put right into the acting, and you would not know me. It makes me laugh to see men and women cry and wipe their noses in the last act . . .

I am going to sing *Faust* in September at Monza, which I hope will go well. Do send the papers oftener. Sometimes it does seem as if I should die off with nothing to read in English. I am obliged to read French and Italian.

I shall hurry home as soon as possible. It is rather lonesome sometimes, I assure you . . .

Next Saturday night is my benefit. I shall sing the Mad Scene from *Lucia* extra. My dresses are all very nice, and I cut a swell. Well, good-night.

It was one o'clock last night when I got to bed.
Lillie

LETTER 14
DO YOU STILL REMEMBER ME?
Yo-Yo Ma to Leonard Bernstein
21 December 1965

At a fundraising event in Washington D.C. on 29 November 1962, in front of a 5,000-strong audience that included President John F. Kennedy, First Lady Jacqueline Kennedy and Dwight D. Eisenhower, an impossibly talented seven-year-old cellist and his sister were introduced as follows by a master of ceremonies who just happened to be the great composer Leonard Bernstein.

An aspect of that double stream of art I mentioned earlier flowing into and out of America, has long been the attraction of our country to foreign artists, and scientists and thinkers, who have come not only to visit us, but often to join us as Americans, to become citizens of what to some has historically been the land of opportunity and to others the land of freedom. And in this great tradition, there has come to us, this year, a young man aged seven, bearing the name Yo-Yo Ma. Now Yo-Yo came to our attention through the great master Pablo Casals who had recently heard the boy play the cello. Yo-Yo is, as you may have guessed, Chinese, and has lived up to now in France – a highly international type. But he and his family are now here. His father is teaching school in New York, and his eleven-year-old sister, Yeou-Cheng Ma, is pursuing her musical studies, and they are all hoping to become American citizens. We shall now have the pleasure of hearing Yo-Yo Ma, accompanied by his sister Yeou-Cheng Ma, play the first movement of the Concertino No. 3 in A Major by Jean-Baptiste Bréval, who played, taught, and composed for the cello 150 years ago in France. Now, here's a cultural image for you to ponder as you listen. A seven-year-old Chinese cellist, playing old French music, for his new American compatriots. Welcome Yo-Yo Ma and Yeou-Cheng Ma.

Three years later, Yo-Yo Ma wrote a letter to Bernstein. He then went on to become one of the most successful cellists of all time.

THE LETTER

21 December 1965

Dear Mr. Bernstein,
Do you still remember me? Now I am ten years old. This year I learned with Prof. Leonard Rose three concertos: Saint-Saëns', Boccherini's and Lalo's. Last week my sister and I played in a Christmas Concert in Juilliard School. We are invited to give a joint recital in Brearley School on January 19, 1966 at 1:45 p.m.

If you have time, I would be glad to play for you.

Yo-Yo Ma

'IF YOU HAVE TIME,
I WOULD BE GLAD
TO PLAY FOR YOU'
— Yo-Yo Ma

LETTER 15
GET AT THE VERY HEART OF IT
Ludwig van Beethoven to Emilie H.
17 July 1812

It was at the beginning of July 1812 that forty-two-year-old German composer Ludwig van Beethoven wrote one of his best known missives: a passionate, ten-page declaration of love to his 'Immortal Beloved' which still to this day provokes discussion, not least due to a recipient whose identity remains a mystery and whom it seems Beethoven was unwilling to live without. A week later, in the wake of such anguish, he was writing an altogether different kind of letter, this time to an eight-year-old girl. Emilie H. was an admirer and aspiring pianist from Hamburg who, with help from her governess, had recently sent to her musical idol a hand-embroidered pocketbook as a thank you for his work. In return, young Emilie received a letter of advice far more honest than one would expect, and a generous invitation to write again.

THE LETTER

Teplitz, 17th July, 1812.

My Dear Good Emilie, My Dear Friend!
I am sending a late answer to your letter; a mass of business, constant illness must be my excuse. That I am here for the restoration of my health proves the truth of my excuse. Do not snatch the laurel wreaths from Händel, Haydn, Mozart; they are entitled to them; as yet I am not.

Your pocket-book shall be preserved among other tokens of the esteem of many people, which I do not deserve.

Continue, do not only practise art, but get at the very heart of it; this it deserves, for only art and science raise men to the God-head. If, my dear Emilie, you at any time wish to know something, write without hesitation to me. The true artist is not proud, he unfortunately sees that art has no limits; he feels darkly how far he is from the goal; and though he may be admired by others, he is sad not to have reached that point to which his better genius only appears as a distant, guiding sun. I would, perhaps, rather come to you and your people, than to many rich folk who display inward poverty. If one day I should come to H., I will come to you, to your house; I know no other excellences in man than those which causes him to rank among better men; where I find this, there is my home.

If you wish, dear Emilie, to write to me, only address straight here where I shall still be for the next four weeks, or to Vienna; it is all one. Look upon me as your friend, and as the friend of your family.

LUDWIG V. BEETHOVEN

'DO NOT ONLY PRACTISE ART, BUT GET AT THE VERY HEART OF IT; THIS IT DESERVES, FOR ONLY ART AND SCIENCE RAISE MEN TO THE GOD-HEAD.'

— Ludwig van Beethoven

LETTER 16
I DON'T EVEN WRITE TO MY MOTHER
Roger Taylor to *Rolling Stone* magazine
1981

In June 1980, British rock band Queen embarked on The Game Tour, a five-leg, eighty-one-gig world tour that lasted until November the next year and included the band's first live shows in South America. It was after one particular show in Buenos Aires that a highly unflattering report appeared in Rolling Stone *magazine that stooped so low as to feature a review not of the concert itself, but of the 'simply awful' sound check. Journalist James Henke also accused the rhythm section of being 'sloppy and sluggish', Brian May's guitar playing as 'boring' and Freddie Mercury's singing 'lackadaisical and without conviction'. The next month, the following letter – originally written in a fit of rage by the band's drummer Roger Taylor on an airline sickness bag – was reprinted in the offending publication.*

THE LETTER

Rolling Stone,
Stunned, shocked, amazed and asleep upon perusal of your "in-depth" story of Queen in South America ("Queen Holds Court in South America," RS 345). I am a member of said group and extremely fucking proud of its music (not all) and its achievements. I don't even write to my mother, since the written word seems worth less in this day of the telephone and publications such as yours and the *National Enquirer*.

Your peculiar 1970-time-warp attitude, coupled with an innate, congenital miscomprehension of rock & roll, continues to fascinate and annoy. Thank you, oh thank you, for the pseudopolitical slant and personal dishonesty that you continue to peddle in your outdated, opinionated, down-home rag.

Thanks also for the finely tuned musical assessment of my group from our sound check! Grow up. You invented the bitterness. I pity you. You suck. You are boring and you try to infect us.

Awaiting your charming review of my current album in about eight months!

ROGER TAYLOR
London, England

LETTER 17
AIDA WILL GATHER DUST IN THE ARCHIVES
May 1872
Giuseppe Verdi, Prospero Bertani and Giulio Ricordi

Since its delayed premiere in 1870 at Cairo's newly-built Khedivial Opera House, Giuseppe Verdi's enduring masterpiece, Aida, *has wowed audiences around the globe in numerous incarnations. But, as with all things, the reaction hasn't always been positive. In May of 1872, having recently travelled twice to watch the opera, a disappointed Italian gentleman named Prospero Bertani decided to write a letter of complaint to Verdi himself and ask for his money back – not just for the show, but for his expenses, too. Amused, Verdi responded by forwarding the letter to his publisher, Giulio Ricordi, with instructions. The end result, as can be seen, was a written promise from Bertani never to watch the opera again. Much to Bertani's dismay, Verdi later arranged for his letter of complaint to be published in a number of Italian newspapers.*

THE LETTERS

Verdi to his publisher, Giulio Ricordi:

St. Agata, 10 May 1872

Dear Giulio,
Yesterday I received from Reggio a letter which is so amusing that I am sending it to you, asking you to carry out the commission I am about to give you. Here is the letter:

Reggio, 7 May 1872

Much honored Signor Verdi,
On the second of this month, attracted by the sensation your opera, "Aida", was making, I went to Parma. Half an hour before the performance began I was already in my seat, No. 120. I admired the scenery, listened with great pleasure to the excellent singers, and took great pains to let nothing escape me. After the performance was over, I asked myself whether I was satisfied. The answer was in the negative. I returned to Reggio and, on the way back in the railroad carriage, I listened to the verdicts of my fellow travellers. Nearly all of them agreed that "Aida" was a work of the highest rank.

Thereupon I conceived a desire to hear it again, and so on the fourth I returned to Parma. I made the most desperate efforts to obtain a reserved seat, and there was such a crowd that I had to spend 5 lire to see the performance in comfort.

I came to the following conclusion: the opera contains absolutely nothing thrilling or electrifying, and if it were not for the magnificent scenery, the audience would not sit through it to the end. It will fill the theatre a few more times and then gather dust in the archives. Now, my dear Signor Verdi, you can imagine my regret at having spent 32 lire for these two performances. Add to this the aggravating circumstance that I am dependent on my family, and you will understand that this money preys on my mind like a terrible spectre. Therefore I address myself frankly and openly to you so that you may send me this sum. Here is the account:

Railroad, going: 2.60
Railroad, returning: 3.30
Theatre: 8.00
Disgustingly bad dinner: 2.00

Twice: 15.90

Total: 31.80

In the hope that you will extricate me from this dilemma,

I am yours sincerely,

Bertani

My address: Bertani, Prospero; Via St. Domenico, No. 5.

Imagine, if to protect a child of a family from the horrible spectres that disturb his peace, I should not be disposed to pay that little bill he has brought to my attention! Therefore by means of your representative or a bank, please reimburse 27.80 lire in my name to this Signor Prospero Bertani, 5 Via St. Domenico. This isn't the entire sum for which he asks me, but . . . to pay for his dinner too! No. He could very well have eaten at home!!! Of course he will send you a receipt for that sum and a note, by which he promises never again to go to hear my new operas, to avoid for himself the danger of other spectres and for me the farce of paying him for another trip [. . .]

Ricordi to Verdi:

> Milan, 16 May 1872

Dear Giuseppe,

As soon as I received your last letter I wrote to our correspondent in Reggio, who found the famous Signor Bertani, paid the money, and got the proper receipt! I am copying the letter and receipt for the newspaper, and I shall return everything to you tomorrow. Oh, what fools there are in this world! But this is the best one yet!

The correspondent in Reggio writes me: "I sent immediately for Bertani, who came to me right away. Advised of the reason for my invitation, he first showed surprise, but then said: 'If Maestro Verdi reimburses me, this means that he has found what I wrote him to be correct. It's my duty to thank him, however, and I ask you to do it for me.'"

This one is even better!

Pleased to have discovered this rarity of the species, I send the most cordial greetings to you and Signora Peppina.

Giulio

Prospero Bertani to Verdi:

15 May 1872

I, the undersigned, certify herewith that I have received the sum of 27.80 lire from Maestro Giuseppe Verdi, as reimbursement of my expenses for a trip to Parma to hear the opera Aida. The Maestro felt it was fair that this sum should be restored to me, since I did not find his opera to my taste. At the same time it is agreed that I shall undertake no trip to hear any of the Maestro's new operas in the future, unless he takes all the expenses upon himself, whatever my opinion of his work may be.

In confirmation whereof I have affixed my signature.

Bertani, Prospero

LETTER 18
PLEASE ADVISE
Teo Macero to various at Columbia Records
14 November 1969

Up until the moment this anxious memo from record producer Teo Macero sped through the offices of Columbia Records in November of 1969, everyone involved in the production of Miles Davis's groundbreaking, genre-redefining, boundary-pushing new album was quite happily under the impression that upon its release it would bear the admittedly bland but mercifully inoffensive name 'Listen To This'. And then Miles Davis called. Presumably the memo's recipients advised Macero to simply accept the demand, for Davis's jazz opus was indeed released to huge fanfare and acclaim four months later, its packaging proudly emblazoned with Davis's inarguably less forgettable title. It is difficult to imagine it any other way.

THE LETTER

CBS MEMORANDUM

FROM: Teo Macero
TO: JOHN BERG, JOE AGRESTI, PHYLLIS MASON
DATE: November 14, 1969

<u>RE: MILES DAVIS CS 9961 XSM 151732/3 PROJECT # 03802</u>

Miles just called and said he wants this album to be titled:

"BITCHES BREW"

Please advise.
    Teo

LETTER 19
DON'T LET ANYONE DEFINE WHO YOU ARE
Angélique Kidjo to Girls of the World
2013

Angélique Kidjo was born in 1960 in the West African city of Ouidah, Benin, and from an early age was immersed in the world of music and dance thanks to her mother, an acclaimed choreographer and theatre director. Influenced largely by traditional folk songs but also by the slices of American rock 'n' roll that made their way across the Atlantic Ocean, in 1989 she released her debut solo album Parakou. *In 1983 she escaped the turbulence of her communist-ruled home country and moved to Paris to study at jazz school, on arrival instantly feasting on all the music she could possibly absorb. In 2013, with thirteen albums under her belt, a Grammy Award to her name, and numerous plaudits for her continued activism, Kidjo chose to impart some hard-earned wisdom to the girls of the world by way of an open letter.*

THE LETTER

Dear Girls of the World,

I was a 12-year-old girl living in the center of Cotonou, Benin, in West Africa. Music was all around us, with the traditional singers and their drums and with the radio blasting songs from the entire world.

Singing had always been my passion. My mom even told me I sung before I spoke. One day, I discovered an uplifting song that made everyone dance. It was called "Pata Pata." The power and beauty of the voice singing it mesmerized me. I had to get the 45 rpm single right away. That's when I first heard the name of Miriam Makeba, the famous South African singer. I also learned her struggle against apartheid and her success all over the planet.

Even though at home I could see the respect that my father had for my mom, I could feel the world was unbalanced and that it was so hard for girls and women to succeed. Many of my girlfriends at school were dropping out at an early age as the social pressure was huge. Most of them could not choose their own destiny. It was as if they would always be the daughter, the wife or the mother of someone.

But looking at Miriam's smile on the cover, her confidence and the respect she inspired, I started to dream. If an exiled African woman born from a poor family had been able to accomplish so much, there might be a little chance for me to follow her steps. Lost in my thoughts, lying on my bed, listening to her music for hours, learning by heart the lyrics of all her songs – in my imagination, I was already traveling with her, singing with her, meeting world leaders and advocating with her for the freedom of her people.

That dream has never left me. I grew up and I experienced much rejection, many obstacles, but Miriam's voice was always singing in my head. I started to have some success singing on the national radio.

One day, on the way back from school, a group of teenagers recognized me and insulted me, calling me a whore because I was a singer. I came back home, crying, and wanted to give up singing for good. Mama Congo, my maternal grandmother, happened to be home. She asked me why I was crying so much. Once I explained, she gave me a piece of advice that I have never forgotten and that I want you to remember when you feel your dreams are shattered.

She told me: "Do you want to be a singer?"

"Yes, Grandma"

"Then, you can't let the opinion of other people discourage you. Don't give up on your dreams, don't allow them to define who you are or they would have won!"

Many years passed. I left my country like Miriam had done. I worked hard, listening to constructive critics and ignoring the naysayers, keeping Miriam's songs close to my heart. Then, in a different decade, in a different country, the day finally came when I was asked to sing as the opening act of my beloved idol. I could not believe it.

Please remember girls: Don't let anyone define who you are!

Angélique Kidjo

LETTER 20
NOT THAT ONE, DOCTOR – IT'S GOT NO RHYTHM
Richard Strauss to Hans Diestel
15 July 1931

In 1931 author Hans Diestel wrote to celebrated German composer Richard Strauss in an effort to gain some expert insight into the world of orchestral music, a subject on which he was soon to publish a book, Ein Orchestermusiker über das Dirigieren. *This fascinating letter, Strauss's reply, ultimately became its preface: a perfect introduction from one of the leading composers of the twentieth century, who wrote his first composition at the age of six and never looked back.*

THE LETTER

Dear Herr Diestel,

When from 1886 to 1889 I first conducted operas as Royal Director of Music in the Court Theatre at Munich (such things still existed in those days with unlimited subsidies and singers without contractual holidays) my father, who was then 65, still occupied his seat as first hornplayer as he had done for 45 years, always arriving from a fabulous sense of duty one hour before the performance was due to begin, concerned not only lest he should bungle his own difficult solo passages in Così fan tutte, but also worried lest his inexperienced son at the conductor's rostrum should make a blunder.

It was at this time that he, who had admired Lachner and opposed Billow, remarked with some irony: "You conductors who are so proud of your power! When a new man faces the orchestra from the way he walks up the steps to the rostrum and opens his score – before he even picks up the baton we know whether he is the master or we."

Using this remark as a motto, as it were, for your book, I would say to my esteemed colleagues: Don't be too proud of your three curtain calls after the third Leonora overture. Down there in the orchestra amongst the first violins, in the back amongst the horns or even at the other end of the timpani there are argus-eyed observers, who note each of your crotchets or quavers with critical regard, who groan if you wave your baton furiously in their faces conducting *Tristan* "alla breve" in four, or when you celebrate the movement "By the Brook" or the second variation in the adagio movement of the "Ninth" by beating twelve complete quavers. They even revolt if you constantly shout "ssh" and "piano, gentlemen" at them during the performance, whilst your right hand constantly conducts forte. They wink if you say at the beginning of a rehearsal "the woodwind is out of tune" but cannot indicate which instrument is playing too high or too low. The conductor up there may imagine that they follow reverently each movement of his baton, but in reality they go on playing without looking at him when he loses his beat and they blame his "individualist interpretation" for every false tempo when he is, let us say, conducting a symphony for the first time which they have played a hundred times before under better conductors.

During one rehearsal when my baton had been mislaid and I was just about to pick up another, the first solo viola player of the Vienna Philharmonic called out to me, "Not that one, Doctor—it's got no rhythm."

In short, the stories of how conductors have been caught out by members of the orchestra would fill volumes. And yet this malicious mob, who plod their weary way in a chronic mezzojorte, who cannot be flattered into accompanying pp or into playing chords in a recitative precisely unless the right man happens to be at the rostrum, with what enthusiasm do they not play—tortured though they be by blunderers with no idea of rehearsing, tired out as they are by giving lessons—with what self-sacrifice do they not rehearse if they know that their conductor will not worry them unnecessarily, how readily will they not obey his slightest gesture on the evening of the performance (especially if he has let them off a rehearsal), when his right hand, fully mastering the high art of conducting, conveys to them his exact intentions; when his eye surveys their playing severely yet benevolently; when his left hand does not form a fist in ff passages and does not unnecessarily restrain them in p passages.

It is simply untrue to say that one can compose "everything," if "composing" be defined as the translation of a sensual or emotional impression into the symbolic language of music. It is, of course, equally true that one can paint in sounds (especially certain movements), but one always runs the risk of expecting music to do too much and of lapsing into sterile imitation of nature. No matter how much intelligence and technical knowledge go into the making of such music, it will always remain second-rate.

I am convinced that the decisive factor in dramatic effect will be a smaller orchestra, which does not drown the human voice as does a large orchestra. Many of our younger composers have already found this out for themselves. The orchestra of the opera of the future is the chamber orchestra which, by painting in the background of the action on the stage with crystalline clearness, can alone realize precisely the intention of the composer with regard to the vocal parts. It is after all an important desideratum that the audience should not only hear sounds but should also be able to follow the words closely.

My conducting has frequently been criticized because, more especially at the beginning, people found fault with the *tempi* of my performances of Beethoven. But I ask, "Who would today assert dogmatically that Beethoven himself wished a tempo to be taken at a particular pace? Is there such a thing as an authentic tradition in such matters?"

There is no such tradition and that is why I hold

that it must be left to the purely subjective artistic acumen of the conductor to decide what is right or wrong. I reproduce every work of Beethoven, Wagner, etc., according to my insight into these works, gained in the course of many years, in the conviction that this is the only true and right way.

Time and again I tried to return to the symphonic literature which has absorbed and fascinated me from my youth. But to this day nothing worthwhile would come into my head. Even program music is only possible and will only be elevated to the sphere of art, if its creator is above all a musician capable of inventing and creating. Otherwise, he is a charlatan, because the quality and cogency of musical invention are the foremost factors even in program music.

It is perhaps due to the spirit of the age that our successors, our "younger generation," our "moderns," can no longer accept my dramatic and symphonic work as a valid expression of the musician and the man in me, which is alive therein, although its musical and artistic problems have as far as I am concerned already been solved at the point at which they begin for "the younger generation." We are all children of our own age and can never jump over its shadow.

Richard Strauss

LETTER 21
PICTURE THE SCENE
Rik Mayall to Bob Geldof
26 November 1984

On 25 November 1984 dozens of the brightest stars on the British music scene descended upon SARM West Studios in London to unite as Band Aid, a supergroup brought together by Bob Geldof and Midge Ure to record the song 'Do They Know It's Christmas?' in a wildly successful effort to raise money for those suffering in the devastating famine in Ethiopia. The day after the recording session, the Young Ones' Rik Mayall (according to his memoir, Bigger than Hitler – Better than Christ*) wrote a letter of complaint to Geldof.*

THE LETTER

Bob Geldof
Basement Flat
126b Kilburn High Road
London NW8

26th November 1984

Dear Bob,
Love you work – or I did until I turned up yesterday at Air Studios to do my bit for Band Aid. What in the name of sweet Fanny fucking Nightingale is going on? All I wanted to do was join my pier group of international stars from the world of pop and rock and record a simple tune which might bring much needed food and provisions to the starving in Africa. But oh no. No, no, no, no, no. Absolutely ruddy bloomin' well not.

Picture the scene. That's the one. There I am walking towards Air Studios just as that Phil Collins is going in. I called to him but he pretended not to hear me. Between you and me Bob, I've never liked him. There's something a bit seedy about him. Something not quite right. And those bloody awful records. Anyway, I was on my way in after him when this enormous bloke in a bomber jacket

blocked my passage. Ooer I thought but figured
this was probably just some sort of joke dreamt up
by one of my great popstar mates like Francis Rossi
or Kool from Kool and the Gang. The bloke said,
"We don't want your sort around here." I laughed
knowingly but he was deadly serious. I told him to
go and tell you that I had arrived and that I had
come to do my bit. When he came back a few
minutes later, he lied and said that he had spoken
to you and you had told him to tell me to fuck off.

It was then that Simon Le Bon arrived with his
all-girl backing band. I called across to him and
told him there had been a horrible mix up but he
pretended he didn't recognise me. What is wrong
with these people? So then I spoke to the big bloke
in the bomber jacket again and it was then that he
beat me up. Yes Bob, perhaps you should read that
sentence again. That's right, I was beaten up at a
charity recording. Your charity recording. How's that
make you feel?

So there I was lying on the pavement when a
limo pulls up next to me and out climbs Boy
George with George Michael and Bananarama and
they all definitely recognised me as they stepped
over me and went inside, even though they
pretended that they didn't. You can just tell.

Undeterred (no offence), I went around to the

back of the building where I managed to find a window that was ajar. I climbed through it and imagine my horror when I fell head first into a toilet bowl. Now you know me Bob, I'm well known for not swallowing, but on this occasion I had been taken by surprise and I managed to swallow about half a gallon of toilet water and something that I can only describe as "solid". This made me feel sick but I decided I would press on and I managed to make my way through to the studio. I'll say this for you Bob, you got some big stars there: Boneo, Paul Wella, Chris Cross – it was wall-to-ceiling talent and just as I was taking in the sheer enormity of it all and chatting star-to-star with various top rock legends like Paul Young, I overheard you tell the security guard to "Get that twat with the shit in his hair out of here." All I can presume is that this was a joke on your part that backfired because the security guard in question did actually throw me out.

Obviously if this is all a great-mates-together music biz joke that you're all playing on me then I want you to know that I'm completely comfortable with that and love everyone as though they were my brother – or sister. But if it isn't, then you're all a bunch of jealous talentless fuck-holes.

And another thing – you should seriously

consider rerouting some of the funds from Ethiopia in order to get yourself some proper professional celebrity endorsement from light entertainment giants like me. You'd make much more money in the long run but you're probably too mean and spiteful to realise it.

Anyway Bob, get back to me. Soon. Say "hi" to Midge,

Rik.

'AND ANOTHER THING —
YOU SHOULD SERIOUSLY
CONSIDER REROUTING
SOME OF THE FUNDS
FROM ETHIOPIA IN
ORDER TO GET YOURSELF
SOME PROPER
PROFESSIONAL CELEBRITY
ENDORSEMENT FROM
LIGHT ENTERTAINMENT
GIANTS LIKE ME.'
— Rik Mayall

LETTER 22
WHO IS KAREN CARPENTER, REALLY?
Kim Gordon to Karen Carpenter
Date unknown

On 4 February 1983, thirty-two-year-old Karen Carpenter passed away after suffering heart failure brought on by anorexia nervosa, an eating disorder with which she had been struggling for a long time. Her funeral, held a week later, was attended by thousands, and with good reason: for fourteen years until her tragic death, Karen had been one half of The Carpenters, a band she had formed with her brother, Richard, in 1969, and which over the years had built up an adoring fan base of millions. Thirty years after her death, Kim Gordon, co-founder of rock band Sonic Youth and a fan of Karen's, wrote her a letter. It was reprinted, undated, in the book Sonic Youth: Sensational Fix.

THE LETTER

Dear Karen,

Thru the years of The Carpenters TV specials I saw you change from the Innocent Oreo-cookie-and-milk-eyed girl next door to hollowed eyes and a lank body adrift on a candy-colored stage set. You and Richard, by the end, looked drugged—there's so little energy. The words come out of yr mouth but yr eyes say other things, "Help me, please, I'm lost in my own passive resistance, something went wrong. I wanted to make myself disappear from their control. My parents, Richard, the writers who call me 'hippie, fat.' Since I was, like most girls, brought up to be polite and considerate, I figured no one would notice anything wrong—as long as, outwardly, I continued to do what was expected of me. Maybe they could control all the outward aspects of my life, but my body is all in my control. I can make myself smaller. I can disappear. I can starve myself to death and they won't know it. My voice will never give me away. They're not my words. No one will guess my pain. But I will make the words my own because I have to express myself somehow. Pain is not perfect so there is no place in Richard's life for it. I have to be perfect too. I must be thin so I'm perfect. Was I a teenager once? . . . I forget. Now I look middle-aged, with a bad perm and country-western clothes."

I must ask you, Karen, who were your role models? Was it yr mother? What kind of books did you like to read? Did anyone ever ask you that question—what's it like being a girl in music? What were yr dreams? Did you have any female friends or was it just you and Richard, mom and dad, A&M? Did you ever go running along the sand, feeling the ocean rush up between yr legs? Who is Karen Carpenter, really, besides the sad girl with the extraordinarily beautiful, soulful voice?

your fan – love,

kim

'DID ANYONE EVER ASK YOU THAT QUESTION— WHAT'S IT LIKE BEING A GIRL IN MUSIC? WHAT WERE YR DREAMS?'

— Kim Gordon

LETTER 23
POPPY-COCK
Harry S. Truman to Paul Hume
6 December 1950

On the evening of 5 December 1950, a carefully selected 3,500-strong audience filled Washington's Constitution Hall to witness a singing performance by Margaret Truman, the only child of US President Harry Truman, also in attendance. Despite the generally held consensus that her singing talents were lacking, a polite wave of positive reaction greeted her after the concert, but not from one person who refused to feign delight – the Washington Post's *music critic, Paul Hume, whose honest review the next morning contained the following:*

> Miss Truman is a unique American phenomenon with a pleasant voice of little size and fair quality [. . .] Miss Truman cannot sing very well. She is flat a good deal of the time – more last night than at any time we have heard her in past years [. . .] There are few moments during her recital when one can relax and feel confident that she will make her goal, which is the end of the song [. . .] Miss Truman has not improved in the years we have heard her; she still cannot sing

with anything approaching professional finish. She communicates almost nothing of the music she presents.

Naturally, her father was livid, and instantly fired off a letter to Hume. The next day, much to Margaret's annoyance, it was front-page news.

THE LETTER

THE WHITE HOUSE
WASHINGTON

Dec. 6. 1950

Mr. Hume:-

I've just read your lousy review of Margaret's concert. I've come to the conclusion that you are an "eight ulcer man on four ulcer pay."

It seems to me that you are a frustrated old man who wishes he could have been successful. When you write such poppy-cock as was in the back section of the paper you work for it shows conclusively that you're off the beam and at least four of your ulcers are at work.

Some day I hope to meet you. When that

happens you'll need a new nose, a lot of beefsteak for black eyes, and perhaps a supporter below!

Pegler, a gutter snipe, is a gentleman along side you. I hope you'll accept that statement as a worse insult than a reflection on your ancestry.

H.S.T.

'SOME DAY I HOPE TO MEET YOU. WHEN THAT HAPPENS YOU'LL NEED A NEW NOSE, A LOT OF BEEFSTEAK FOR BLACK EYES, AND PERHAPS A SUPPORTER BELOW!'

— Harry S. Truman

LETTER 24
THE COLOR OF THE STARS, HER SKIN, HER LOVE
Jon M. Chu to Coldplay
8 December 2017

Upon its hugely successful record-breaking release in 2018, the movie Crazy Rich Asians *drew praise from far and wide, not just for being an entertaining piece of cinema, but also for being the first Hollywood film in a quarter of a century to boast an all-Asian cast. Then there is the soundtrack. As the film ends, a woman begins to sing Coldplay's hit song 'Yellow', but in Mandarin rather than English. During production of the film, its director Jon M. Chu was adamant that Coldplay's song feature, but his request to use it was denied. Undeterred, Chu wrote this letter to the band. Within days, he was given the green light.*

THE LETTER

December 8, 2017

Dear Chris, Guy, Jonny and Will,
I know it's a bit strange, but my whole life I've had a complicated relationship with the color yellow. From being called the word in a derogatory way throughout grade school, to watching movies where they called cowardly people yellow, it's always had a negative connotation in my life. That is, until I heard your song. For the first time in my life, it described the color in the most beautiful, magical ways I had ever heard: the color of the stars, her skin, the love. It was an incredible image of attraction and aspiration that it made me rethink my own self image. I remember seeing the music video in college for the first time time on TRL. The one shot with the sun rising was breathtaking for both my filmmaker and music-loving side. It immediately became an anthem for me and my friends and gave us a new sense of pride we never felt before . . . (even though it probably wasn't ever your intention). We could reclaim the color for ourselves and it has stuck with me for the majority of my life.

So the reason I am writing this now, is because I

am directing a film for Warner Bros. called CRAZY RICH ASIANS (based on the best selling novel) and it is the first ALL-ASIAN cast for a Hollywood studio film in 25 years. Crazy. We were recently featured on the cover of Entertainment Weekly to commemorate this fact. The story is a romantic comedy about a young Asian-American women (played by Constance Wu) from New York coming to terms with her cultural identity while she's visiting her boyfriend's mother (played by Michelle Yeoh) in Singapore. It's a lavish, fun, romantic romp but underneath it all, there's an intimate story of a girl becoming a woman. Learning that she's good enough and deserves the world, no matter what she's been taught or how she's been treated, and ultimately that she can be proud of her mixed heritage. The last scene of the movie shows this realization as she heads to the airport to return home a different woman. It's an empowering, emotional march and needs an anthem that lives up and beyond her inner triumph, which is where **Yellow** comes in. It would be such an honor to to use your song that gave me so much strength throughout the years, to underscore this final part of our film. And for me personally, it would complete a journey that I've been going through, fighting to make it in the movie business.

I know as an artist it's always difficult to decide when it's ok to attach your art to someone else's—and I am sure in most instances you are inclined to say no. However, I do believe this project is special. I do believe this is a unique situation in which the first Hollywood studio film, with an All-Asian cast is not playing stereotypes or side-players, but romantic and comedic leads. It will give a whole generation of Asian-Americans, and others, the same sense of pride I got when I heard your song. I know it's recontextualized but I think that's what makes it powerful. I want all of them to have an anthem that makes them feel as beautiful as your words and melody made me feel when I needed it most.

Your consideration would mean so much to me and our project.

I can show you the movie if you want to see the context, or talk to you if you have any questions. Thank you for taking the time to listen.

Much love,

Jon M. Chu

Director of Crazy Rich Asians

LETTER 25
IT'S A VIRUS
Tom Waits to *The Nation*
July 2002

When, in 1988, Tom Waits heard what seemed to be his own voice singing on a Doritos commercial broadcast to the nation, his first thought was to question his own sanity. Then, very quickly, he became furious. It soon transpired that Frito-Lay, Inc. had hired a Tom Waits impersonator to bring the advert to life, perfectly imitating the gravel-voiced musician in a bid to sell snacks – a situation Waits could not abide. A lawsuit ensued, at the end of which he was awarded $2m. In 2002, fourteen years after that advert first pricked his ears, Waits read an article in The Nation *by The Doors' John Densmore on the subject of musicians allowing their work to be featured in commercials. Tom Waits responded with this letter.*

THE LETTER

Woodland Hills, Calif.

Thank you for your eloquent "rant" by John Densmore of The Doors on the subject of artists allowing their songs to be used in commercials.

Songs carry emotional information and some transport us back to a poignant time, place or event in our lives. It's no wonder a corporation would want to hitch a ride on the spell these songs cast and encourage you to buy soft drinks, underwear or automobiles while you're in the trance. Artists who take money for ads poison and pervert their songs. It reduces them to the level of a jingle, a word that describes the sound of change in your pocket, which is what your songs become. Remember, when you sell your songs for commercials, you are selling your audience as well.

When I was a kid, if I saw an artist I admired doing a commercial, I'd think, "Too bad, he must really need the money." But now it's so pervasive. It's a virus. Artists are lining up to do ads. The money and exposure are too tantalizing for most artists to decline. Corporations are hoping to hijack a culture's memories for their product. They want an artist's audience, credibility, goodwill and all the energy the songs have gathered as well as given over the years. They suck the life and meaning from the songs and impregnate them with promises of a better life with their product.

Eventually, artists will be going onstage like race-car drivers covered in hundreds of logos. John, stay pure. Your credibility, your integrity and your honor are things no company should be able to buy.

TOM WAITS

'REMEMBER, WHEN YOU SELL YOUR SONGS FOR COMMERCIALS, YOU ARE SELLING YOUR AUDIENCE AS WELL.'

— Tom Waits

LETTER 26
HERBS IS HIS MAJESTY'S
Lee 'Scratch' Perry to Tokyo's Minister of Justice
21 January 1980

During a luggage check on 16 January 1980, as Paul McCartney entered Japan, customs officials found 7.7 ounces of cannabis among his belongings – a haul that could have led to years in prison, but which, luckily for the Beatle, resulted in a nine-day stay in a Tokyo prison and the cancellation of an eleven-city Wings tour of Japan. He was deported upon release and warned never to return. Prior to this slap on the wrist, fans all over the globe feared the worst for Macca, and messages of support materialised from far and wide. But the highlight of the whole ordeal came five days into his incarceration, when his friend – the eccentric inimitable reggae legend that is Lee 'Scratch' Perry – wrote a letter to Tokyo's Minister of Justice in an effort to lend his support.

THE LETTER

21 JANUARY 1980

ARK OF THE COVENANT
5 CARDIFF CRESENT DR.
KINGSTON, JAMAICA
AIR WHITE SMOKE SIGNAL
EARTH MOON BASE
JUDA ONLY LAW HOUSE
ISREAL LIGHT HOUSE

MINISTER OF JUSTICE
1-1-1 KASUMIGASEKI
CHIYODA-KU
TOKYO, JAPAN

Dear Sirs,
I LEE PIPECOCK JACKSON PERRY would LOVE to express my concern over your consideration of one quarter kilo to be an excessive amount of herbs in the case as it pertains to master PAUL McCARTNEY.

As a creator of nature's LOVE, light, life and all things under the creation sun, positive feelings through songs, good times and no problems. I find the Herbal powers of marijauna in its widely recognized abilities to relax, calm and generate positive feeling a must.

Herbs is his Majesty's. All singers positive directions and liberty Irrations. Please do not consider the amount of herbs involved excessive.

Master PAUL McCARTNEY's intentions are positive.

BABY BLUE GREEN STAR
PIPECOCK JACKSON
LEE "SCRATCH" PERRY
BANNANA EYE I PEN JA
NATURES LOVE DEFENDER

LETTER 27
A HARMONIOUS CREATION OF ART
Adele aus der Ohe to Steinway & Sons
1894

From a very young age, Adele aus der Ohe was a remarkable pianist. Born in Hanover in 1861, she was just ten years old when she performed her debut concert; by the age of twelve she had been taken under the wing of Franz Liszt, the Hungarian virtuoso with whom she would continue to study for seven invaluable years. Later on in life she performed at Carnegie Hall with her friend and mentor, the Russian composer Pyotr Ilyich Tchaikovsky, and later played piano at his funeral. During the course of her incredible career she played with the Boston Symphony Orchestra more than fifty times. She performed to crowds all over the world. She also composed. All told, Adele aus der Ohe was a musician of the highest order.

In 1894, she wrote a letter of appreciation to Steinway & Sons, the manufacturers of her favoured grand piano.

THE LETTER

New York,
1894

Messrs. Steinway & Sons

Gentlemen:

It gives me great pleasure to express my admiration for your pianos. Their tone is noble, sonorous and pure; even in the utmost fortissimo, it is rich and sweet; moreover, it carries so far that it makes the most delicate pianissimo practicable in very large halls. The tone is not only large and round, but exquisitely sensitive and fresh. These qualities make the Steinway piano better adapted to cantabile playing at one extreme and to the most passionate bravoura at the other, than any other piano that I know. The scale is very even in the best sense of the word:- the bass rich and pure, the treble singing and full, the upper octaves round and replete with vitality and character.

The action of the Steinway piano, combining, as it does, depth, power, lightness and elasticity, affords the artist the means of producing the most delicate shades of tone-color, the most piquant effects and the most tremendous bravoura.

The Steinway piano is, in brief, a harmonious creation of art so individual and sympathetic that the artist often feels as if it possessed a living personality of its own.

With my kind regards,
Yours very sincerely,
Adele aus der Ohe

LETTER 28
PLEASE CHANGE YOUR HOLD MUSIC
Dr Steven Schlozman to CVS
May 2018

As Assistant Professor of Psychiatry at Harvard Medical School and a psychiatrist at Massachusetts General Hospital, Dr Steven Schlozman spends an inordinate amount of time on the phone to CVS, a pharmaceutical behemoth whose retail stores have reached all corners of the United States since the company was founded in 1963. Frustratingly for Dr Schlozman, for the past twenty years CVS have neglected to refresh the hold music which greets those who call for healthcare assistance, instead offering up the same piece of piano music each and every time a customer calls. In May 2018, at his wit's end, Dr Schlozman wrote to them with a plea which, thanks to the power of the Internet, was soon read by millions.

Ten months and much coverage later, CVS announced that plans were underway to install a new telephone system.

THE LETTER

Dear CVS,

Please change your hold music.

Please. Do the right thing.

It'll take you, or someone who works for you, or even a barely pubescent adolescent who nevertheless knows how to program music on his iPhone with more aplomb than anyone born before 1975, only about 48 seconds.

And 48 seconds is substantially less than the amount of time I have listened to your never-changing hold music.

I have researched the source of this music online. I did this, as you might guess, when I was on hold. It seemed the healthiest response I could muster to that faux-soothing piano wandering that is supposed to placate customers for anywhere between 20 seconds and 35 minutes.

I am just guessing at these wait times, by the way. That data might be out there and it might not, but I can't bring myself to see how long my waiting compares to the average waiting.

And, to be clear, I am not critical of being on hold. I know the pharmacists are working as hard as they can. I know it's part of our modern world. This is why we have social media, and ESPN.com, and trashcans placed about four or five feet away, into which I can toss crumpled-up pieces of paper. In fact, being on hold has greatly improved my trashcan basketball accuracy, so there's that. Thank you.

Still, that tune has got to go.

I hear it in my sleep. I hear it when I go running. Sometimes I wake in the middle of the night humming that melody. It haunts me, day and night. It's not healthy. I know. I'm a doctor.

It's not healthy to hear pharmacy-hold music while you sleep.

Oh, you want data?

Fair enough.

CVS hold music stimulates the almond-shaped amygdala that sits in our reptilian brains, and that's not good. This is the same region of the brain involved in road rage, and in raising your middle finger, and in listening to the Steve Miller Band sing "Abracadabra."

Some 98 percent of respondents in a large, multi-center study examining the average American's response to the CVS pharmacy hold music reported that their amygdalae (the plural of amygdala) were enraged.

This study, obviously, does not exist. But it could!

The subjects would be made up entirely of me, or lots of me's. You see, there are many, many different me's that have listened to that same tune while on hold at CVS. There's the me who is in-between patients and operating under the resilient but nevertheless largely naive belief that I can solve a prior authorization quandary in somewhere around four minutes. There's the me, nervous about my daughter's ear infection, and hoping that the antibiotics are ready. There's the me doing laps in my car around and around the street where I live, waiting for the music to end so that I can talk to an organic entity and call in a prescription.

As for numbers, I've got those figured out as well.

Let's say I call CVS, on average, three times per day, six days a week, for a period of about the last 25 years. That would allow me to count my residency as well as post-graduate years. Let's subtract a couple weeks a year for holidays and so forth.

That means that three times per day, six days a week, 50 weeks a year for 25 years, I've called CVS. And let's estimate that the average time that I am treated to this music is around 1 minute, 34 seconds.

That means that I have made approximately

22,500 calls to CVS, and I am, in all honesty grateful for their service. (6 x 3 x 50 x 25 = 22,500)

Of course, I am making an assumption that the hold music has not changed over the last 25 years. This is because I don't recall it changing. It's like taxes. I don't remember a time when it didn't exist. Accepting this assumption as fact — because it *feels* like fact — this means that I have listened to roughly 2,115,000 seconds of that same music. That's 35,250 minutes, or 587-1/2 hours, or nearly 25 days.

Almost 25 days of my life listening. I am 52 years old, so that means that I have spent 25 days out of my 18,980 days on this planet listening to that piano piece (called, incidentally, "Golden Dragon" — I Googled it while I was on hold). That's a higher percentage of my days than I'd like.

So let me be clear. I don't object to being on hold. I hate it, but I am at peace with it. I object to being on hold for more than 587 hours of my hard-earned life while listening to that same tune.

As I hope this piece illustrates, this is a matter of some urgency.

Please change the music.

Please.

With warmest regards,

Steve

'IT'S NOT HEALTHY
TO HEAR PHARMACY-
HOLD MUSIC WHILE
YOU SLEEP.'

— Dr Steve Schlozman

LETTER 29
BLOW 'EM AWAY, KID
Nick Cave to Ptolemy
2019

Nick Cave's long and illustrious music career began in 1973 with the formation of his first band, The Boys Next Door, which soon became The Birthday Party, a post-punk outfit which lasted a decade before being replaced by Nick Cave & the Bad Seeds. Cave has also produced multiple film scores and written two novels, an epic prose poem called The Sick Bag Song *and a number of award-winning screenplays. Most recently he has curated* Stranger than Kindness, *a multi-media exhibition of his work and influences. In 2018 he launched The Red Hand Files, a platform through which members of the public are able to ask questions of him directly. In 2019, he responded to a letter from Ptolemy, a young fan living in Launceston, Australia, who had asked:*

> I am 10 and have been surrounded by and listened to your music as long as I can remember. I saw you in Hobart in January 2017 and I'll be there again to see you in January 2019. None of my friends listen to anything cool, interesting or beautiful. How will having your music in my life so early on affect me, and have you got any advice for me?

THE LETTER

Dear Ptolemy,

I think I may have already answered your question at the In Conversations in Hobart – if you're the little blonde kid, who was sitting on the right side of the hall. I can't remember exactly what I replied, but I thought more about the question after the show, and I remember wishing I had answered it better.

Perhaps, this is what I should have said. Listening to Bad Seeds music at your age is like having a secret knowledge. When I was about your age I had a secret knowledge too. My eldest brother, Tim, used to listen to a lot of very strange and obscure music and he passed this knowledge on to me. Back then I lived in a rural city in Victoria and it seemed to me that nobody my age listened to the music my brother played to me. As far as I could tell they all listened to a whole lot of shit. It was like I carried a secret around inside me, a special knowledge about the world that my friends didn't have. It was a secret power. I carried this secret power with me all through my kid-years until I went to a school in Melbourne, where I met three or four other people who also had this special knowledge – this secret power. These people became my best friends and we went on to form a band and tried, in our way, to take this knowledge and pass it on to the world.

This secret knowledge you have is a strength that lives only inside certain people. It is a strength that will inspire you to do wondrous things – like write stories, or draw pictures, or build rockets that fly to Mars. It will give you the courage to take on anything that the world might put in front of you. It's a wild power that can be of untold value to the world. Your name, Ptolemy, is a warrior's name. A boy full of inspiration with a warrior's name! The world is waiting for you. Blow 'em away, kid.

Love, Nick.

LETTER 30
THE CREATIVE URGE
John Coltrane to Don DeMichael
2 June 1962

As a saxophonist, bandleader and composer, John Coltrane will forever remain a giant in the world of jazz, a community that owes so much to his innovative, instantly recognisable sound. Born in 1926 in North Carolina, it was a stint in the Miles Davis band in the 1950s that forced people to take notice of his talents, but it was his solo releases – including his 1960 masterpiece, Giant Steps, that truly thrust him into the spotlight and etched his name into the very fabric of jazz history. Two years after the release of Giant Steps, Coltrane was sent, by the editor-in-chief of Downbeat magazine Don DeMichael, a copy of Music and Imagination, a book containing a series of lectures delivered by composer Aaron Copland at Harvard University in 1951. This letter was Coltrane's response.

THE LETTER

June 2, 1962

Dear Don,

Many thanks for sending Aaron Copland's fine book, "Music and Imagination." I found it historically revealing and on the whole, quite informative. However, I do not feel that all of his tenets are entirely essential or applicable to the "jazz" musician. This book seems to be written more for the American classical or semi-classical composer who has the problem, as Copland sees it, of not finding himself an integral part of the musical community, or having difficulty in finding a positive philosophy or justification for his art. The "jazz" musician (You can have this term alog with several other that have been foisted upon us.) does not have this problem at all.

We have absolutely no reason to worry about lack of positive and affirmative philosophy. It's built in us. The phrasing, the sound of the music attest this fact. We are naturally endowed with it. You can believe all of us would have perished long ago if this were not so. As to community, the whole face of the globe is our community. You see, it is really easy for us to create. We are born with this feeling that just comes out no matter what conditions exist. Otherwise, how could our founding fathers have produced this music in the first place when they surely found themselves (as many of us do today) existing in hostile communities when there was everything to fear and damn few to trust. Any music which could grow and propagate itself as our music has, must have a hell of an affirmative belief inherent in it. Any person who claims to doubt this, or claims to believe that the exponents of our music of freedom are not guided by this same entity, is either prejudiced, musically sterile, just plain stupid or scheming. Believe me, Don, we all know that this word which so many seem to fear today, "Freedom," has a hell of a lot to do with this music.

You know, Don, I was reading a book on the life of Van Gogh today, and I had to pause and think of that wonderful and persistent force — the creative urge. The creative urge was in this man who found himself so much at odds with the world he lived in, and in spite of all the adversity, frustrations, rejections and so forth — beautiful and living art came forth abundantly . . . if only he could be here today. Truth is indestructible. It seems history shows (and it's the same way today) that the innovator is more often than not met with some degree of condemnation; usually according to the degree of his departure from the prevailing modes of expression or what have you. Change is always so hard to accept. We also see that these innovators always seek to revitalize, extend and reconstruct the status quo in their given fields, wherever it is needed. Quite often they are the rejects, outcasts, sub-citizens, etc. of the very societies to which they bring so much sustenance. Often they are people who endure great personal tragedy in their lives. Whatever the case, whether accepted or rejected, rich or poor, they are forever guided by that great and eternal constant – the creative urge. Let us cherish it and give all praise to God. Thank you and best wishes to all.

Sincerely,
John Coltrane

'WE ARE BORN WITH THIS FEELING THAT JUST COMES OUT NO MATTER WHAT CONDITIONS EXIST.'

— John Coltrane

PERMISSION CREDITS

Every effort has been made to trace copyright holders and obtain their permission for the use of copyright material. The publisher apologises for any errors or omissions and would be grateful if notified of any corrections that should be incorporated in future reprints or editions of this book.

LETTER 1 Copyright © Mindless Records, LLC, 2010. Extracted from Life by Keith Richards (Published in 2010 by Weidenfeld & Nicholson) / Reproduced with permission of Curtis Brown Group Ltd, on behalf of Keith Richards / From Life by Keith Richards, copyright © 2010. Reprinted by permission of Little, Brown and Company, an imprint of Hachette Book Group, Inc.

LETTER 4 Copyright © 2016, Leonard Cohen, used by permission of The Wylie Agency (UK) Limited.

LETTER 5 Reprinted by kind permission of Mark Taubert.

LETTER 7 Reprinted by kind permission of Ms. Hammond and Mr. Taylor, grandchildren of Florence Price. Letter is located in the Library of Congress, Music Division, Serge Koussevitzky Archive.

LETTER 8 An open letter to Miles Davis by Charles Mingus November 30, 1955 Downbeat Magazine.

LETTER 9 Reprinted by kind permission of Billy Altman literary executor of the Estate of Lester Bangs.

LETTER 12 ©Yoko Ono Lennon – Used by permission/all rights reserved.

LETTER 14 Reproduced by kind permission of Yo-Yo Ma.

LETTER 16 Reprinted by kind permission of Roger Taylor.

LETTER 18 Teo Macero Collection, New York Public Library for the Performing Arts.

LETTER 19 Reprinted with kind permission of Angélique Kidjo, Grammy Award-winning singer-songwriter and UNICEF Goodwill Ambassador.

LETTER 21 Reprinted by permission of HarperCollins Publishers Ltd © (2005) (Rik Mayall).

LETTER 22 Reprinted by kind permission of Kim Gordon.

LETTER 24 Reprinted with kind permission of Jon M. Chu.

LETTER 25 Tom Waits Letter, © 2002, Tom Waits. Courtesy of Jalma Music. Used By Permission. All Rights Reserved.

LETTER 26 Reprinted with permission of Canongate Books Ltd. Copyright © 2000 David Katz. With thanks to Lee 'Scratch' Perry.

LETTER 28 Reprinted with kind permission of Dr. Steven Schlozman.

LETTER 29 Nick Cave on The Red Hand Files reproduced by kind permission of Nick Cave.

LETTER 30 © Jowcel Music, LLC. Used by Permission / All Rights Reserved.

ACKNOWLEDGEMENTS

It requires a dedicated team of incredibly patient people to bring the Letters of Note books to life, and this page serves as a heartfelt thank you to every single one of them, beginning with my wife, Karina – not just for kickstarting my obsession with letters all those years ago, but for working with me as Permissions Editor, a vital and complex role. Special mention, also, to my excellent editor at Canongate Books, Hannah Knowles, who has somehow managed to stay focused despite the problems I have continued to throw her way.

Equally sincere thanks to all of the following: the one and only Jamie Byng, whose vision and enthusiasm for this series has proven invaluable; all at Canongate Books, including but not limited to Rafi Romaya, Kate Gibb, Vicki Rutherford and Leila Cruickshank; my dear family at Letters Live: Jamie, Adam Ackland, Benedict Cumberbatch, Aimie Sullivan, Amelia Richards and Nick Allott; my agent, Caroline Michel, and everyone else at Peters, Fraser & Dunlop; the many illustrators who have worked on the beautiful covers in this series; the talented performers who have lent their stunning voices not just to Letters Live, but also to the Letters of Note audiobooks; Patti Pirooz; every single archivist and librarian in the world; everyone at Unbound; the team at the Wylie Agency for their assistance and understanding; my foreign publishers for their continued support; and, crucially, my family, for putting up with me during this process.

Finally, and most importantly, thank you to all of the letter writers whose words feature in these books.